Contents

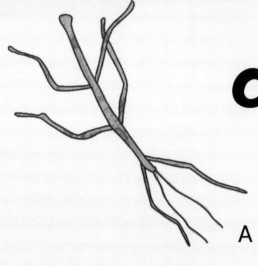

A Note About Nature

Planet Earth is home to a mind-boggling diversity of life. It is beautiful, awe-inspiring, unexpected, joyful, unbelievable, and sometimes just plain weird.

This book is a tribute to some of these characteristics. In the poems and rhymes on the following pages you will find surprising facts and scientific descriptions, but hopefully you will also encounter a love of the natural world that will make you want to go out and learn, explore, and play more with nature.

Some poems are long, while some are very short, and there are lots of different rhyming patterns, as well as several non-rhyming Haikus.

A Haiku is a beautifully simple yet profound form of poetry that originated in Japan. It consists of three lines of verse where the first line has five syllables, the second has seven, and the last has five again. They are traditionally little sonnets to nature, and you will appropriately find quite a few throughout this book. Why not try writing one or two yourself once you've found them all?

You can read this book in whatever way you like. Feel free to dip in and out or simply read it through from cover to cover. But bear in mind that, just like when we're out there exploring the natural world in real life, you might find some treasures in unexpected places if you stay open-minded and choose to linger and ponder things for a little longer than you normally would.

Above all, remember that we are not outside observers of the natural world. We are part of the amazing wild world of living creatures that share this planet, and we have a role to play in it.

Tremendous Trees

Amazing Fact!

The Tallest tree in the world is a Coast Redwood in California called Hyperion. Redwoods typically grow to about 300 feet in height, which is roughly the same as a 25-storey building. But Hyperion has reached an incredible 379 feet (115m). The oldest individual trees in the world are also found in California and Nevada, where some Bristlecone Pines have been dated at around 5,000 years old.

Tall Trees

Tall trees in the woods,
Swaying in the gentle wind.
Majestic and grand.

To Be A Tree

Someday soon I hope to be,
As strong and true as you, dear tree.
My feet on the ground, my head in the sky,
At one with the world as it rolls by.

To feel the breeze, to taste the sun,
To live the seasons one by one,
To watch the day from start to end,
To know the birds and bugs as friends.

My feet on the ground, my head in the sky,
At one with the world as it rolls by.
Someday soon I hope to be,
As strong and true as you, dear tree.

What Is A Tree?

A tree is a plant like so many others,
With roots and leaves just like its plant brothers.
It still needs sun and soil and rain.
It blooms anew each spring again.
It filters the air, as most plants do,
Giving life and breath to me and you.

But trees are plants that are tall and high,
Reaching up towards the sky.
Each has a solid central stem,
A trunk it's called, and each of them,
Is wrapped in bumpy patterned bark,
And from them graceful branches arc,
Fanning out their leaves of green.
The finest sight you've ever seen.

Trees are home to countless bugs,
Birds and fungi, bats, and slugs.
Trees are worlds of life diverse,
Each a sprawling universe.
Each a rare and precious thing,
Because of all the life they bring

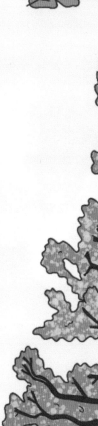

Between the worlds of earth and air.
They're like a bridge, or bond, or stair.
Stretching up and stretching down,
Brushing clouds and piercing ground.
Ancient yet young, wise yet new.
A symbol of life and all that's true.

Stick

I found a stick and picked it up
and walked with it a while.
We hiked and trekked,
explored at length, for mile after mile.

I found a stick and picked it up
and swung it round and round,
I fought with dragons, beasts
and every monster that I found.

I found a stick and picked it up
and stuck it in the ground.
I grew a beanstalk up it,
twirling round and round.

I found a stick and picked it up
and then I found some more.
I built a fort to keep me safe
from bandits, storms, and war.

4

I found a stick and picked it up
and waved it with a flair,
Transforming rocks and casting spells,
with magic in the air.

I found a stick and picked it up
and took it to a brook.
I set it free, it raced away,
without a backwards look.

I found a stick and picked it up
and played and played and played.
We adventured, we imagined,
through rain and sun and shade.

Precious Plants

Amazing Fact!

The largest flower in the world is the Rafflesia Arnoldii which can be over 3 feet (1m) across. Unfortunately, it is also one of the smelliest flowers in the world with an odor like decaying flesh so that it can attract the flies that pollinate it. It is found in the rainforests of Borneo and Sumatra in southeast Asia and is appropriately known as the corpse flower or stinking corpse lily.

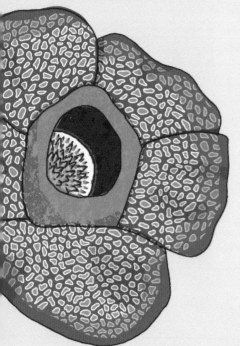

Plant Power

Plants all have a special power,
like nothing else on earth.
A unique magic talent
that is gifted them at birth.
Other creatures hunt and chase,
tracking down their food.
Or search or dig or forage,
being clever, sharp and shrewd.
But plants just stretch out in the sun,
basking in its light.
The chlorophyl within them,
glowing deep and green and bright.
Harnessing this chemical,
the plant makes its own food,
Add some soil-y goodness
and the plant can be renewed.

Mossy Magic

Moss, oh moss, so green and bright,
Growing soft in morning light.
A carpet of life upon the ground,
In every corner moss is found.

Tiny leaves like furry fluff.
On rocks and trees, there's room enough,
For all to grow and fill this place.
A world of green and endless grace

Mossy banks by riverside,
A cool and calming place to hide.
In the damp and misty air,

A world of wonder dwelling there.
Mossy forests cloak the earth,
A haven for new life and birth.
Lichens and fungi side by side,
In natural tapestry reside.

So, come and explore this natural treasure,
Moss, the green and growing pleasure!
A carpet of life upon the ground,
In every corner moss is found.

Beautiful And Bright

A flower in spring,
Beautiful and bright it blooms,
And scent fills the air.

A Seed

A seed germinates.

A seed germinates,
the rain waters it,
and a root grows down.

A seed germinates,
the rain waters it,
a root grows down,
a stem grows up,
and leaves emerge.

A seed germinates,
the rain waters it,
a root grows down,
a stem grows up,
leaves emerge,
a flower blooms,
and the bees come and go.

A seed germinates
and the rain waters it.

A seed germinates,
the rain waters it,
a root grows down,
and a stem grows up.

A seed germinates,
the rain waters it,
a root grows down,
a stem grows up,
leaves emerge,
and a flower blooms.

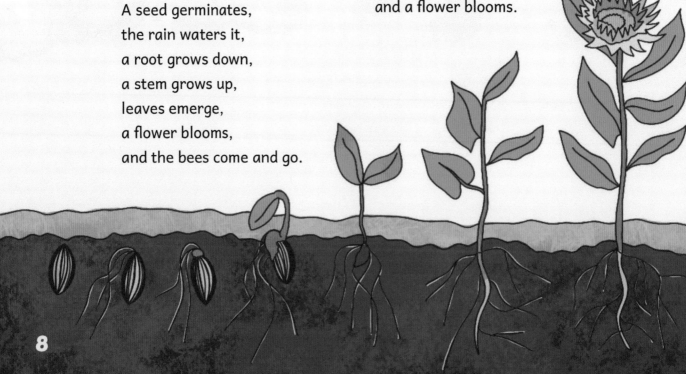

Precious Plants

A seed germinates,
the rain waters it,
a root grows down,
a stem grows up,
leaves emerge,
a flower blooms,
the bees come and go,
and the flower is transformed
to fruit to seeds.

And the seeds disperse.
And a seed germinates

Fantastic Fungi

Amazing Fact!

What we think of as a mushroom is in fact just the 'fruit' of a much larger organism. This fruit that blooms above ground allows it to disperse spores and reproduce. But the underground mycelium structure, made up of twisted strands called hyphae, can spread over incredible distances. The largest continuous individual mushroom, found in Oregon, USA, is estimated to cover an area of 3.5 square miles.

Sprawling

Fungi fill our world.
Sprawling through the damp and dark,
Weird and wonderful.

Hey, Mushroom!

Hey, mushroom, are you a plant?
No, I'm not, you see I can't...

I can't be a plant. Take a look – just use your eyes.
I don't have plant-y bits and can't photosynthesize.
I am not green and have no leaves for drinking rays.
That's not how I make my food. No, I have other ways.

Roots though, you have those, don't you?
No, I don't, that's not quite true...

A root grows slowly, and it works like a straw.
It sucks up water from the earthy floor.
I have hyphae, in fact they're most of me.
They search around for rotting things and munch for my tea.

Not a plant, so what are you?
Here, let me explain to you...

There's a kingdom for the plants, and one for animals,
That's the one for crabs, for birds, for humans, and for camels,
But me and all my relatives like truffles, yeast and mold,
Are the kingdom of the Fungi – it is noble, great and old.

Noble? But you're just a fungus!
Though we're small, our role's humungous!

We make things decompose, so they break down and then decay.
Without us dead things simply would not, could not, go away.
There'd be bodies everywhere and no room left for life.
If we did not do our thing, oh, think of all the strife!

Wow Mushroom, I never knew!
The planet owes so much to you.

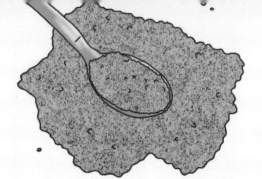

A Fabulous Fungus

Oh, sweet and bubbly, brilliant yeast!
You're such a magnificent magical beast,
Essential to my crusty feast.
Making my bread rise

Without you, we're at an impasse,
You eat the sugar, produce the gas,
You make the doughy gloopy mass,
Swell to twice its size.

You're tiny, small, almost invisible,
Yet mighty, strong, almost invincible,
In making bread, oh so delectable,
It's you that makes the difference.

So, thank you, yeast, for all you do,
For buns and baps and baguettes too.
You fabulous fungus, three cheers to you,
For all your baking brilliance!

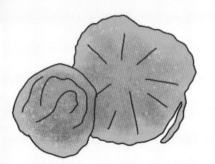

A Lament Of Mold

Mold, oh mold, must you attack,
Turning all things green and black?
From dark damp corners, you come creeping,
Expanding out while we lay sleeping.
Unleashing spores that make us wheeze,
That make us ill and spread disease.

You have some use, I must admit.
In making cheese, you are a hit.
And in medicine you have your role.
But I'm afraid that, on the whole,
I'd rather keep you out of sight.
So, stay away... if that's alright.

Magestic Mammals

Amazing Fact!

The largest animal to have ever lived is a mammal. The Blue Whale takes the crown as it can reach 98 feet (30m) in length and weigh up to 150 tons. These incredible animals were once found in oceans around the world but were almost hunted to extinction until the killing of Blue Whales was banned by the International Whaling Commission in 1966. However, they are still endangered due to other human actions such as pollution and climate change.

What Is A Mammal?

Mammals come in such variety of species,
And they're found all over the Earth.
But in certain ways they're all alike,
Starting with how they give birth.

They all give birth to live young babies...
Wait – that's not quite true.
Echidnas and the platypus,
Are mammals, but lay eggs – they do!

But mammals all do this for sure:
Mothers make milk for their young
Even the ones that hatch from eggs,
This is still how it's done.

Mammals all have hair or fur...
Apart from one or two.
Whales, dolphins, porpoises don't,
And elephants barely do.

Giraffe

Graceful towering,
Eating leaves from high treetops.
Proudly standing tall.

But mammals all do this the same:
They keep warm on their own.
This means they're quite adaptable,
Making anywhere their home.

They dont need the sun's warm rays,
To warm their blood inside.
Their bodies do that on their own,
Even when it's cold outside.

There's other little things as well,
Making mammals all the same:
Like three bones in the middle ear,
A neocortex in the brain.

But mammals are so varied,
In their shapes and lives and sizes.
Each unique and beautiful,
And full of wild surprises.

15

Brilliant Bears

There are many different types of bear,
Each with its own unique flair.
Each adapted to the lands they roam,
To make the most of their own home.

Polar bears in snow and ice –
With their thick coats it's rather nice.

The grizzly brown bear, big and strong,
With teeth and claws so sharp and long.

The Indian sloth bear, slow and steady,
Who only moves when necessary.

The sun bear, always on the go,
A curious, speedy, little fellow.

The giant panda, black and white –
Bamboo is their one delight.

The black bear, who can climb so high,
And forage for bugs so small and sly.

The spectacled bear, who got his name,
From his golden fur with eyeglass frame

There's a bear for almost everywhere,
A furry, fabulous, brilliant bear!
Each adapted to the lands they roam,
To make the most of their own home.

A List Of Interesting Mammals

Ring-tailed lemurs, kangaroos,
Elephants and elephant shrews.

Rhinos, horses, mice, wombats,
Three-toed sloths and jungle cats.

Badgers, hedgehogs, rabbits, hares,
Mountain gorillas, polar bears.

Flying squirrels, buffaloes,
Dolphins, fruit bats, armadillos.

Bandicoots and manatees,
Otters, wolves, and chimpanzees.

Pumas, narwhals, lions, gerbils,
Dingoes, hamsters, skunks and mandrils.

Tigers, reindeer, cows, warthogs,
Pandas, whales, and all pet dogs.

And of course, there's me and you.
Humans. Yes, we're mammals too!

Brilliant Birds

Amazing Fact!

Dinosaurs are not extinct. You might have thought that was a typo, so let's repeat it: Dinosaurs are not extinct! Dinosaurs are animals whose legs protrude downwards from their bodies (instead of sideways as they do for reptiles) and are covered in scales or feathers. So, birds are in fact dinosaurs! It's thought that birds evolved from feathered dinosaurs much like small velociraptors, who walked on their hind legs, during the Jurassic period.

Our Chicken Overlords

There's more than
twenty-five billion chickens,
Around the world today.
I'm afraid that they might actually,
Get organised one day.
You see, they outnumber
human beings,
By more than three to one!
If they rise up,
then before you know it,
Revolution has begun!

Birds

Birds are all so feathery,
With wings to soar so high and free,
(Though some just stick to earth and sea),
But all start life as eggs.

With special bones to aid with flight,
Birds can reach tremendous height,
With air-filled bones to make them light,
And all start life as eggs.

Their varied beaks suit what they eat:
Nectar, fish, or seeds, or meat.
Birds all stand on two clawed feet,
And all start life as eggs.

Each bird has some distinctive call:
Some chirp, some sing, some caterwaul,
Some screech, some wail and that's not all,
But all start life as eggs.

Birds build many varied nests.
Some strive to make their nest the best,
So a female might choose it from the rest,
Then there she'll lay her eggs.

An egg is such a such a wondrous thing,
Perfect protection for the gift within,
A symbol for life about to begin,
For all birds come from eggs.

The Tiniest Bird

Hummingbird in flight,
Flitting amongst the flowers,
The tiniest bird.

Flightless Birds

Some wings are of little use,
Too small, or weak, or feathers too loose.
Yet these birds can still get by,
They walk or swim where others fly.

To find their food and find their mate,
These birds just walk and that works great.
They may not have the gift of flight,
But they can run and swim and fight.

Ostriches, emus, rhea, and kiwis,
All types of penguin and cassowaries.
There's others too, like the Kakapo.
Chickens? Well, they have a go.

Still, they get where they need to go,
And they're quite happy going slow.
For they are masters of their world,
These flightless birds with wings unfurled.

Magical Molluscs

Amazing Fact!

Molluscs are incredibly varied. Most species have some sort of shell (although slugs, octopuses and some others don't) and most are marine creatures (although slugs and snails are not). It's quite hard to define what makes a mollusc a mollusc in any simple way because they come in such an incredible array of shapes and sizes. In fact, there may be over 100,000 different species of mollusc out there!

The Octopus

Like writhing dancers, they glide about,
Poets of movement and motion,
Artists of most tranquil enchantment,
From the very depths of the ocean.

They are beings of wonder and mystery,
Alert with keen sensations.
Intelligent marvels of the seas,
Fantastical creations.

In the watery depths they lurk,
Ready to jump out and snare,
Any unsuspecting prey,
Fish and crabs beware!

Molluscs

Most molluscs are soft-bodied, but with a shell,
A shell that's a home, and protection as well,
The shell can be round, or flat or spiralled,
Colorful, plain, or incredibly detailed.

Most molluscs have one very muscular foot,
Under the body is where this is put.
A mantle secretes its hard outer shell,
A digestive tract is in there as well.

A mollusc has also a specialized tongue,
This organ – a radula – gets the work done,
It can scrape, and rasp, to grind up its food,
So it can be nourished, fed and renewed.

A mollusc's a creature, so strange and wondrous,
From so many places and endlessly curious.
It comes in all sorts of shapes and sizes,
Weird and varied, full of surprises.

Patient Mollusc

Hiding in the sand,
The peaceful clam is waiting,
For the tide to come.

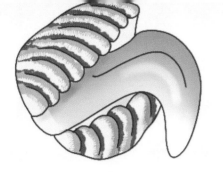
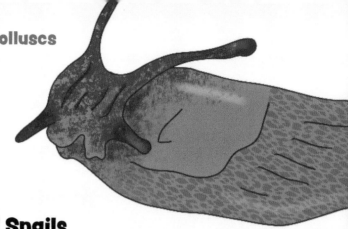

Slugs And Snails

Slugs and snails, they slide and crawl,
Leaving slimy trails that sprawl,

On leaves and grass they love to dine,
Moving slowly, all the time.

With shells or not, they roam around,
Sliding over soggy ground,

Leaving mucus as they go,
As they slither to and fro.

In gardens, they are rarely liked,
In fact, they cause a lot of strife.

But, they keep the plants in line,
Holding back marauding vines

And, they're sluggy, snaily feasts,
Nutritious meals for many beasts.

Though small and slow, they've got their place,
In naturc's grand and diverse space.

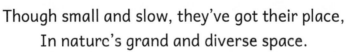

Fabulous Fish

Amazing Fact!

When we think of fish we think of fins, scales, being cold-blooded and breathing water. Most fish do have fins (although hagfish and lampreys technically don't) but there are actually quite a few species of fish that have leathery skin instead of scales. There is even one special family of fishes – Opah or sunfish – who can regulate their own body temperatures like mammals and birds. The most defining thing about fish is that they can all breathe in water. They still need oxygen, but they get this from water by sucking it in through their mouths and filtering it out through their gills. Even mudskippers, who are able to crawl out of water, breathe through water stored in their gills and through their wet skin, so they still have to stay constantly moist.

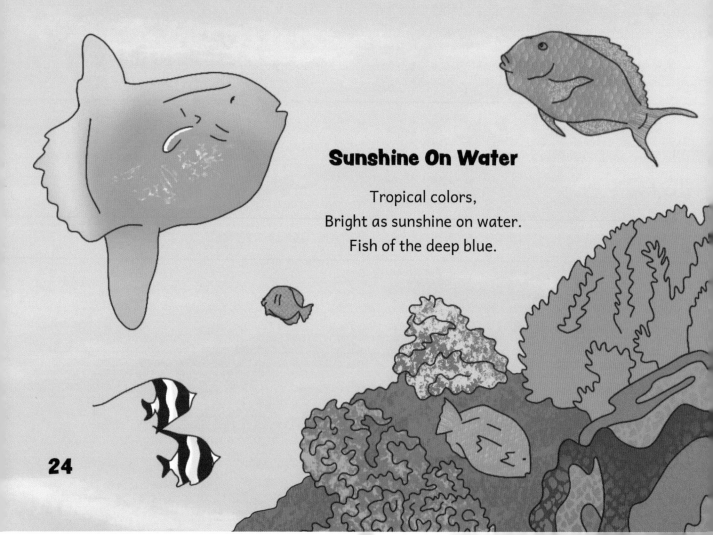

Sunshine On Water

Tropical colors,
Bright as sunshine on water.
Fish of the deep blue.

Seahorses

A Seahorse is a graceful thing,
Almost dancing as it swims.
And though it has a horsey face,
It never gets to trotting pace.

They're not built for racing wins,
Propelled by rather little fins.
There's no need to rush or speed.
They mostly drift to what they need.

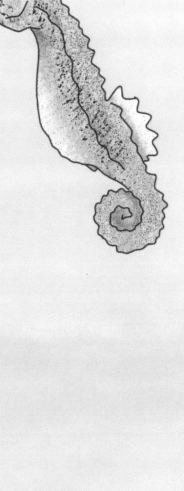

With coiling tail, so sleek and long,
Elegant but also strong,
They grasp on tight to reeds below,
Holding fast against the flow.

They mate for life, so seahorse pairs,
Don't have many courtship cares.
They live lives of wedded bliss,
Don't we all want lives like this?!

And when it's time to lay their eggs,
They're carried by the dad instead.
For weeks he keeps them safe and warm,
Until the little fry are born.

(It makes you think of seafood dishes,
But Fry's the name for baby fishes.
Perhaps these baby fish should be,
Seafoals instead – don't you agree?!)

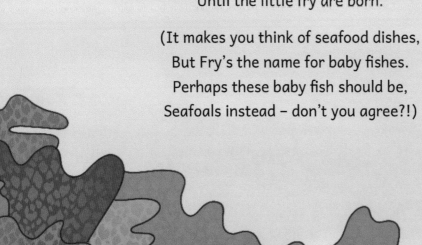

Fish Can Be...

Fish can be dull, or bright as the stars,
Blue or red or green,
Silver or gold or black or white,
Or anything in between.

Fish can be long, fish can be short,
Or flat, or fat, or thin.
Fish can be spiky, fish can be smooth,

Fish can have scales or skin.

Fish can have wings and leap in the air,
Or stay on the dark ocean floor.
Fish can live all on their own,
Or in shoals of thousands or more.

Fish can have rows of razor-sharp teeth,
While some fish don't even have jaws.
Some even use their fins like arms,
And haul themselves onto the shores.

Fish, fish, fabulous fish,
Living the life aquatic.
Filling our oceans and rivers with life,
Let's face it, you guys are fin-tastic!

Sharks

Sharks, the ferocious rulers of the seas,
Filling other creatures with dread.
Sleek and swift in search of prey,
That they can rip to shreds.

They've been around for millions,
And millions of years,
And still, they're apex predators,
The ghosts of fishy fears.

But truly, do we need to fear them?
Are they all that bad?
Could they be misunderstood?
They do look rather sad.

Their fearsome rep precedes them,
But they play a crucial role:
Predators keep the delicate balance,
In habitats they patrol.

Let's not forget, the seas are theirs.
Let's just respect their place.
Not think of them as enemies,
When we invade their space.

We share this earth with sharks and more,
Some dangerous, it's true.
But they're not just mindless killing machines,
They're amazing creatures too.

Sharks are ancient, majestic and grand.
They're powerful and strong.
Sharks deserve to be understood,
Then we just might get along.

Remarkable Reptiles

Amazing Fact!

The longest-living species of land animal is a reptile. Giant tortoises can live up to 150 years or more! They can also survive without eating or drinking for up to a year because they can store water and food in their bodies, which helps them survive during the tough times in the wild. In the course of their long lives, they get to grow VERY big, often heavier than a grand piano! They're also incredibly strong. With their powerful legs and strong shells, these tortoises can knock down trees and push boulders out of their way.

What Is A Reptile?

What makes a reptile a reptile, you ask?
For starters they sit in the warm sun and bask.

They can't warm their bodies themselves you see.
They're cold-not-warm-blooded, unlike you and me.

Their skin is all dry, and it's covered with scales.
They scuttle and crawl. They have wriggling tails.

They have earholes, not ears, but they still have good hearing,
So they know when their favourite snack foods are nearing.

Their legs – if they have them – stick out at the sides.
(Snakes don't have any, which helps them to slide.)

Their eggs – if they lay them – are soft little ones.
(But boas and vipers give birth to live young.)

Reptiles breathe air – they have lungs and not gills.
And they're all good at staying remarkably still.

Crocodiles, tortoises, lizards and more.
They've been around since the dinosaurs.

Still going strong in the lands that they roam.
Sharing with us, this earth – their home.

Turtle Teacher

Graceful in the ocean depths,
The turtle glides with ease.
From shallow shores to deepest blue,
Roaming free as the breeze.

Scales that shimmer in the sun,
Its flippers are its wings.
Soaring through its watery world,
At one with everything.

It rides the ocean currents,
Moving through the salty tide.
Always steady, never rushing,
The ocean is its guide.

This ancient soul lives decades long,
A nomad of the sea.
For millions of years it's been like this,
Turtles roaming free.

So why are they in trouble now,
When humans rule the Earth?
Have we forgotten something?
Have we neglected something's worth?

Let's learn from this wise creature,
And treat the ocean realms with care.
For the turtle is our teacher,
And its wisdom we must share.

Dragons

Dragons are real. They are. It's true!
Though they're not quite the fairytale beasts.
These lizards can't fly, and they don't breathe fire,
But they're big and eat dragon-y feasts.

The Komodo Dragon is fast and fierce,
With sharp teeth, and claws so strong.
With powerful legs and a powerful tail,
They grow to be ten feet long.

They've no need for fire when hunting for food,
Their venomous bite does the trick.
They love hunting big things like deer and wild pigs,
They'd even eat you, so run – quick!

Snake

Slithering serpent,
Sleek body and flicking tongue,
Cunning predator.

Amazing Amphibians

Amazing Fact!

When you think of amphibians you probably think first of frogs and toads, but salamanders (including newts) also make up a huge number of amphibian species. And what remarkable amphibians these are. If a salamander loses a leg or tail, it can grow it back. That's right - these amazing amphibians have the ability to regrow body parts, including internal organs and entire limbs, that have been damaged or lost. Scientists are studying salamanders to learn more about regenerative medicine in the hope that this could one day could help humans.

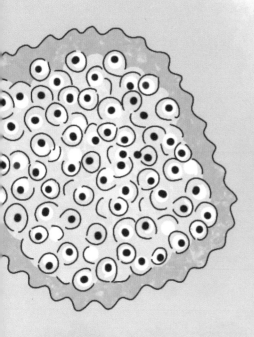

Creature Of Two Realms

An amphibian.
Creature of water and land.
At home in both realms.

Dual Nationality

Amphibians: creatures with dual nationality.
Life in water and on land is, for them, normality.
They breathe through lungs, but also through their skin,
Which is always kept moist whichever place they're in.

Generally, they lay their eggs (lots of them!) in water,
And their polliwog sons and polliwog daughters,
Hatch and spend their childhood living happy lives aquatic,
Eating lots and growing big... then something quite dramatic!

They grow some legs (some lose their tails) then venture out on land.
Now they creep, and leap, and walk, and hop, and crawl and stand.
Still, they love the water too, and swim and duck and dive,
But now they have two options. There's two places they survive.

Such amazing animals amphibians are:
Frogs and toads and salamanders – every one a star.
Amphibians: creatures with dual nationality.
Life in water and on land is, for them, normality.

Frog Or Toad?

Frogs and toads, oh what a sight!
Both amphibians, but not quite alike.

Frogs have smooth and slimy skin,
Toads have bumps, and they're a bit less thin.

Frogs love to swim and jump for joy,
With Toads you find that crawling's their ploy.

Frogs have long legs for leaping high,
Toads have short legs for ambling by.

Frog feet are webbed for swimming around,
Toad feet are better for burrowing down.

Frogs lay their eggs in a big squishy blob,
Toads make strings – a much neater job.

There's more to learn, but this is a start.
Now you know how to tell them apart.

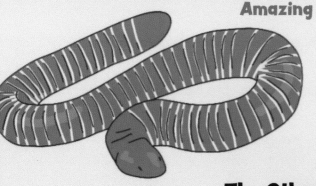

The Other Amphibian

Frogs and toads are quite well known,
As present-day amphibians.
Of course, there's salamanders too,
But don't forget Caecilians.

These guys are always overlooked,
But perhaps that's no surprise.
They live completely underground,
And have no use for eyes.

They look like little snakes or worms,
And live in tropical lands.
Burrowing their days away,
In streambeds, under sand.

So don't forget caecilians.
They're amphibians too,
Just like their cousin newts and frogs.
Give these guys their dues!

Impressive Insects

Amazing Fact!

Scientists estimate that there are over 1 million different species of insects, and that means that there is an incredible diversity amongst them. Some insects have incredible superpowers: The flea can jump up to 200 times its own body length – if a human could do that, we would be able to jump over a 40-story building! And the dragonfly can fly backwards, hover in the air, and even fly upside down! Insects have evolved some seriously impressive abilities to help them survive and thrive in their environments.

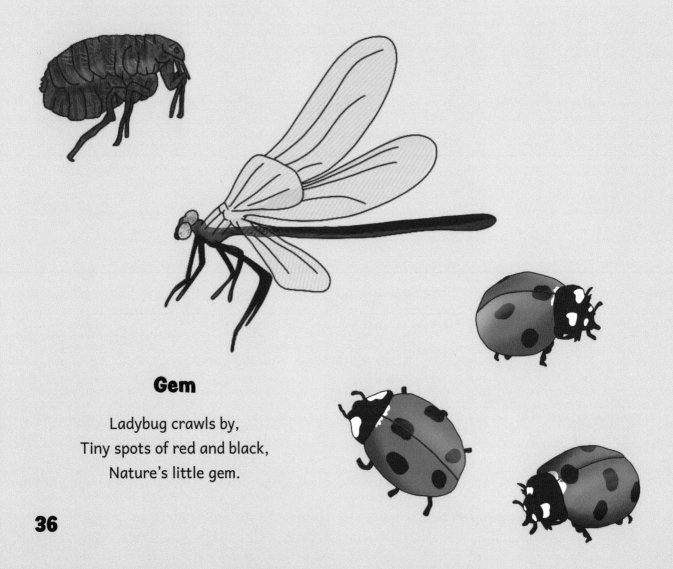

Gem

Ladybug crawls by,
Tiny spots of red and black,
Nature's little gem.

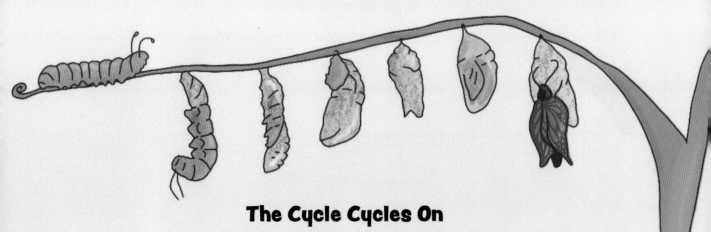

The Cycle Cycles On

Everybody knows the cycle of a butterfly:
First egg then caterpillar, chrysalis then by and by,
The adult can emerge and stretch its wings into the sky.
But lots of other insects do the same.

More than seventy per cent of insects have a cycle too:
Eggs hatch out as larvae and these grubs just need to chew.
They turn into pupae who lie still – that's all they do,
But inside they are brewing up a change.

When the pupa's finished, metamorphosis complete,
The adult's fully grown and then the next part's rather neat.
You see this four-stage cycle is on infinite repeat.
It just keeps going round and round and round.

The adult finds a mate. They lay more eggs and after this.
It's larva.. pupa... adult... and if nothing goes amiss,
The cycle cycles on in a rotating kind of bliss.
In insect species life cycles abound.

Insects Only Have Six Legs

Insects are all arthropods,
but not vice versa, see:
Ticks and spiders are not insects,
nor are centipedes.

Insects only have six legs.
Almost all have wings.
Insects have three body parts,
Unlike these other things.

Spiders and ticks are arachnids,
with abdomens and heads.
But they don't have a thorax,
and they have two extra legs.

Insects only have six legs.
Almost all have wings.
Insects have three body parts,
Unlike these other things.

Similarly centipedes have,
not six legs, but more.
The same applies to millipedes –
they have legs galore!

Impressive Insects

Insects only have six legs.
Almost all have wings.
Insects have three body parts,
Unlike these other things.

A scorpion's an arthropod –
an arthropod that stings!
But still, they have too many legs,
and they don't have wings.

Insects only have six legs.
Almost all have wings.
Insects have three body parts,
Unlike these other things.

All these bugs have things alike.
They're distantly related.
They all have exoskeletons but,
as previously stated...

Insects only have six legs.
Almost all have wings.
Insects have three body parts,
Unlike these other things.

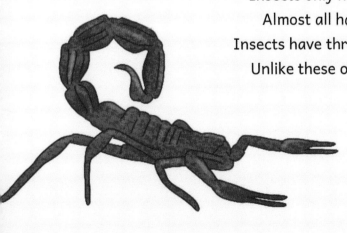

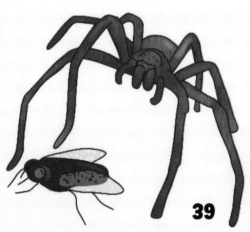

39

Extraordinary Earth

Amazing Earth

It's extremely hard to measure accurately (and scientists' estimates are constantly changing due to evolution, extinction and simply changes in the way we classify things) but it's thought that there are about one and a half million different species of animal in the world today.

Over a million of these are invertebrate species (such as insects, arachnids and molluscs) but there are also more than 5,000 species of mammals, over 6,000 species of amphibians, around 8,000 species of reptiles, more than 10,000 species of birds and roughly 50,000 species of fish.

There are also nearly half a million different species of plant in the world, including all the species of mosses and liverworts, and almost 150,000 species of fungi. These are all estimates, but one thing we know for sure is that there are thousands and thousands of as-yet-unknown species out there, still to be discovered.

One very interesting measure of life on Earth is biomass, which basically means adding up the weight of different groups of creatures so that we can compare them. So, a hive of 100,000 bees, who only weigh about 0.125g each will have a greater biomass than a human toddler.

In terms of biomass, plants make up over 80% of all life on Earth, bacteria make up more than 10% but all animals (of which we are only a fraction) put together make up less than half a percent.

That might make humans seem quite insignificant, but no other species has a greater impact on our planet – for good or for bad – than humanity. And it's a little scary to think that the biomass of humans is about ten times as much as all the wild land mammals in the world put together. It kind of makes you wonder about the balance of things, doesn't it?

But people can make a positive difference... especially you.

We live in a time where humans are really beginning to understand the effect we have on the world, and many, many people are choosing to make a more positive impact. You can recycle, use non-polluting ways of getting around, plant trees, and think carefully about how the food, clothes and other consumables you use are produced. And there are so many more ways of making sure you live in a way that doesn't harm the planet.

Earth's biodiversity is so special and wonderful. As the 'dominant' species, humanity has a responsibility to protect and nourish that, but we need to also remember that we are not outside of nature – we are part of it.

We have a place in the beautiful balance of life.
Let's cherish that and live up to the responsibility.

Balance And Love

Let me tell you a tale of this Earth's magic,
Where every creature and plant is fantastic.
From the oceans deep to the tallest trees,
Each with a role to nurture and please.

Each creature big, each creature small,
Has a purpose, and benefit to all.
Biodiversity is the key,
To a world that's bright and good and free.

So, let's protect each wondrous thing,
And all the life and breath they bring.
For when we find balance, and when we find love,
Our Earth will thrive, below and above.

Printed in Great Britain
by Amazon

33164783R00030